I Live Here Now

by Cam Gregory

Focus Points
Family

I come from Japan.
I live here now.

I come from Mexico.
I live here now.

I come from Somalia.
I live here now.

I come from Pakistan.
I live here now.

I come from Israel.
I live here now.

I come from Iraq.
I live here now.

I come from Korea.
I live here now.

I come from Italy.
I live here now.